A TEMPLAR BOOK

Published in the United States in 1996 by THE MILLBROOK PRESS, INC.
2 Old New Milford Road, Brookfield, CT 06804.
Devised and produced by The Templar Company plc,
Pippbrook Mill, London Road, Dorking, Surrey RH4 1JE, Great Britain.

Designed by Mike Jolley
Printed and bound in Italy

Library of Congress Cataloging in Publication Data
Palin, Nicki.
(Hidden Pictures)
Nicki Palin's hidden pictures: find a feast of camouflaged
creatures / written by A. J. Wood ; illustrated by Nicki Palin.
p.   cm
"A Templar book" – T.p. verso.
Includes bibliographical references (p.   ).
Summary: A puzzle guide to the world's wild places in which the reader
is asked to find a series of animals hidden in their natural habitats.
ISBN 1-56294-369-3 (lib. bdg.) 1-56294-267-0 (trade)
1. Camouflage (Biology) – Juvenile literature.   [1. Camouflage
(Biology)   2. Picture puzzles.]   I. Wood, A. J., 1960-
II. Title.
QL767.W66   1996
591.57'2 – dc20   95-42305   CIP   AC
1 3 5 4 2

NICKI PALIN'S HIDDEN

Written by

A.J. WOOD

Illustrated by

NICKI PALIN

THE MILLBROOK PRESS
Brookfield, Connecticut

PICTURES
FIND A FEAST OF CAMOUFLAGED CREATURES

All over THE PLANET EARTH

there are animals. Some live in lush jungles or quiet woodlands, others in the darkest depths of the deepest oceans, the hottest deserts, or the coldest icecaps. Travel anywhere in the world and you will find them. Some of these creatures will be easy to spot. Walk through a meadow and you may see birds flying overhead, a rabbit scampering for its burrow, an insect feeding from a flower. But what else goes unseen? All around you, countless other creatures will be hiding.

It is the same with this book. Look at the orchids on the opposite page. Can you find three animals concealed somewhere there? Look hard and you should be able to see a fish (look at the leaves), a mouse (look at the spotted pattern on the petals), and a flying bird (look at the space *between* the leaves). Now you're ready to start the hidden picture hunt!

Turn the pages and tour the world. You'll find all sorts of animals waiting to be discovered and, remember, there are more animals hiding from you somewhere within each of Nicki's lovely paintings. See how many you can spot. Then turn to the back of the book to find out more about some of the fascinating creatures that share our world.

**As** FAR AS THE EYE CAN SEE the great plains of Africa stretch away to the horizon. They are home to a diverse group of animals, many of which are camouflaged to help them in their fight for survival. See if you can spot these five striped or spotted animals in the picture.

1. Cheetah
2. Giraffe
3. Zebra
4. Leopard
5. Saw-scaled adder

At THE EDGE OF THE WOOD

a group of animals gather in the early morning sunshine. A hedgehog forages for worms amongst the autumn leaves, observed by a watchful fox. The shrill song of a robin breaks the silence and the sound of a woodpecker's drumming echoes across the wooded valley. See how many other creatures you can spot in the picture, and don't forget to look for these six hidden animals:

1. Fox cub
2. Deer
3. Wren
4. Wood mouse
5. Common toad
6. Woodpecker

Danger ON THE REEF

Coral reefs are colorful places. Almost everything looks as though it has been freshly painted by Mother Nature in the most striking patterns and brightest colors. Fish dart everywhere, decked out in stripes and spots. Luminous sea slugs glide across the coral along with vivid blue starfish. At first sight it might look like it would be fun to live there – but beware! Around every corner danger lurks. See if you can spot these five animals that are best left alone!

1. Shark   2. Moray eel   3. Octopus   4. Stingray   5. Jellyfish

Swampland

The tropical mangrove swamps of the Everglades stretch for miles across the state of Florida in southeastern United States. Peer among the overhanging branches and you might spot a brown pelican or a roseate spoonbill waiting patiently to catch a fish supper, or a colorful lizard on the run from a dangerous snake. In this picture, another hunter is on the look-out for something to eat too. See if you can spot it, along with four creatures that just might be on tonight's swampland dinner menu!

1. Alligator   2. Catfish   3. Turtle
4. Tree frog   5. Salamander

The LOST CONTINENT

Until 1820 no human being had set foot on the great ice continent of Antarctica. It is the coldest and most isolated place on Earth and contains 90% of the world's ice. Virtually no insects or plants can survive on land here, but beneath the waves it is a very different matter. The icy seas teem with life of all kinds and, when summer comes for a few brief weeks, the Antarctic coasts provide a breeding ground for hundreds of different seals and sea birds. In many ways, this is a home of giants. The biggest animal ever to have lived on Earth, the blue whale, swims in the Antarctic seas. The wandering albatross comes here to nest, casting a shadow over the oceans with its enormous wings. And the great bull elephant seal, the world's largest seal, bellows to his rivals across the ice.

But have you noticed one well-known group of animals missing from the picture? Antarctica is also home to literally hundreds of penguins, including, of course, the biggest of them all. See if you can spot five different kinds hiding somewhere in the picture.

Danger IN THE DESERT

Australia's deserts cover more than two thirds of the continent. They are home to many poisonous insects and reptiles, but some of the most fearsome-looking creatures, like this frilled lizard, are really not dangerous at all. In fact, the biggest danger is the lack of water, since in most places less than 10 inches (25 centimeters) fall every year.

Many of the animals of the outback are unique to Australia. Nowhere else on Earth will you find a magnificent red kangaroo, or a frightening frilled lizard. However, this island continent has also become the adopted home of several creatures from elsewhere in the world. See if you can spot these five interlopers:

1. Camel   2. Rabbit   3. Wild horse   4. European mouse   5. Cane toad

Snow WHITE!

Imagine a land so cold that the ocean around it freezes solid, a land where in winter it is dark for 24 hours a day. That is what life is like within the Arctic Circle, a great area of land and sea surrounding the North Pole. Many creatures migrate here in the summer when huge numbers of insects provide a much-needed food supply. But the polar bear lives here all year round. Like many other animals of the Arctic, the polar bear is pure white. See if you can spot six other creatures that, like him, are hard to see against the snow.

1. Snowy owl
2. Ptarmigan
3. Snow bunting
4. Ivory gull
5. Snow goose
6. Arctic tern

Small SURPRISES IN ASIA

Far out to sea, between the great continents of Asia and Australia, lie the islands of the East Indies. With their strings of volcanoes, rushing rivers and miles of lush forest, they are home to a rich and varied range of wildlife, including over 30,000 different kinds of plants. The animals that live here are some of the most impressive and curious in the world – from the world's largest lizard (the Komodo dragon) to the extraordinary orangutan and the majestic tiger. Deep in the rainforests you can also find elephants, rhinos, and tapirs, not to mention over 1,500 species of birds. Look closer and there are a multitude of smaller surprises in store too, for these islands have perhaps the richest insect life of anywhere in the world. From lunar moths and atlas beetles to giant stick insects and beautiful swallowtail butterflies, the forest abounds with fluttering, scuttling, creeping creatures. See if you can find these five hiding from you amongst the undergrowth opposite:

1. Praying mantis   2. Lunar moth   3. Atlas beetle

4. Dragonfly   5. Ant

Land
OF THE CONDOR

The great mountain range of South America, the Andes, stretches for over 5,000 miles (8,000 kilometers) down the western length of the continent. With their snow-capped peaks and glacial lakes, these mountains are home to a strange selection of creatures that have adapted to survive in this harsh climate. Many, like the alpaca and vicuna, have developed thick woolly coats to keep out the cold. And they are so nimble-footed that they can leap with ease over slopes so steep that most other animals would fall to their death. At the top of the mountain the winds are so strong that only the Andean condor, a giant among birds, can still fly.

You can see some of the Andes' native creatures here, but can you spot the condors? There are five hiding somewhere in the picture.

Deep IN THE JUNGLE

all is still. Suddenly, a leaf stirs. A beautifully colored jaguar comes strolling fearlessly through the undergrowth of the Brazilian rainforest. He stops, lifts his head to sniff the air, and lets out a deep-throated growl that breaks the stillness.

Within moments, the jungle is alive with movement and color. A pair of scarlet macaws swoop up to a new perch. A troop of monkeys jump from tree to tree, chattering in a playful game. Brilliant hummingbirds probe deep within the forest flowers in search of nectar, while a pygmy anteater searches for a termite dinner. The picture is completed when the world's slowest animal, the three-toed sloth, reveals itself with a gentle movement as it idles along a branch.

The forest abounds with life. Look again at the picture and see how many animals you can spot, and this time you don't get any help! Just remember, there are more creatures hiding from you than you may think.

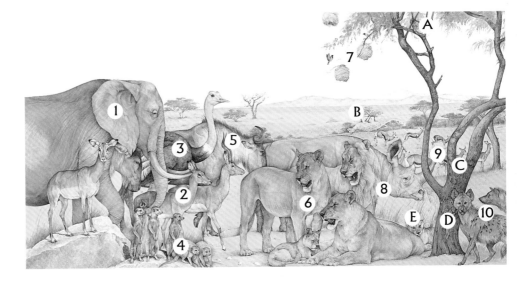

THE AFRICAN PLAINS

As FAR AS THE EYE CAN SEE

The hidden animals

A. Giraffes are the tallest creatures on earth, towering up to 19.5 feet (6m).

B. Cheetahs are the fastest of the big cats, able to reach speeds of 69 miles (112km) per hour.

C. Saw-scaled adders are responsible for more deaths from snake bite than any other species in North Africa.

D. Leopard. Like the cheetah, the leopard's spotted coat helps to camouflage it against its background.

E. Zebras live in family groups, sometimes gathering together in large herds.

What else can you see?

1. African elephants use their trunks for gathering food and also to drink, smell and fight. The young remain with their mothers for several years after birth.

2. Impala. This graceful animal can leap up to 33 feet (10m) – a useful skill in a landscape populated by predators where the impala is always on the look-out for danger. It even gives birth during the hottest part of the day when most predators are asleep.

3. Ostrich. Too big to fly, the ostrich has become an expert runner. Faster than anything else on two legs, it can reach speeds of up to 44 miles (70km) per hour. Its eggs, too, are record-breakers – 40 times larger than the average hen's egg, they are the largest laid by any bird.

4. Meerkats are gregarious animals, living in family groups of up to 30 individuals.

5. Wildebeests may be seen in the tens of thousands, crossing the savannah in giant herds. Like many other plains animals, wildebeests migrate with the changing seasons, often traveling over 1,000 miles (1,600km) to find food.

6. Lion. Impressive hunters, lions spend most of the time asleep. For only a few hours a day will they search the plains for prey, stalking through the long grass before making the final deadly pounce. Lions usually hunt in groups and will band together to attack larger animals such as giraffe, buffalo and even crocodiles.

7. Weaver bird. Expert builders, these birds live in colonies and may build up to 100 nests in the same tree.

8. White rhinoceros. Despite its name, the white rhino usually ranges in color from pale gray to reddish-brown, depending on the color of the mud in which it wallows. It is the second-largest living land animal after the elephant.

9. Thomson's gazelle. The gazelle's markings help to confuse its predators. If disturbed, the whole group will jump into the air in all directions – a jumbled mass of brown, black and white.

10. Hyena. These carnivores will scavenge from the kills made by other animals, but are also powerful hunters in their own right, banding together in packs to attack zebras and antelopes.

At THE EDGE OF THE WOOD

THE EUROPEAN WOOD

The hidden animals

A. Common toad. To help protect it from predators, the toad can ooze poison through glands in its warty skin!

B. Wood mouse. See 9 below.

C. Woodpecker. See 1 below.

D. Deer. The shy deer usually comes out only at dusk to browse on the leaves of shrubs and trees.

E. Wren. The male wren builds several nests of twigs and moss for his mate to choose from. He then lines the selected one with hair and feathers.

F. Fox cub. See 6 below.

What else can you see?

1. Great spotted woodpecker. This bird bores its long beak into tree trunks in search of insects. In spring it drums its beak against the bark for a different reason – to attract a mate.

2. Rabbits live in big family groups, sometimes of up to 100 individuals.

Together, they dig a maze of burrows called a warren. They will graze nearby, constantly sitting up on their hind legs to check for danger, warning each other of approaching enemies by thumping the ground with their hind feet.

3. Robin. The colorful robin is a fierce defender of its territory. It will try to frighten away rivals by puffing out its red breast and singing loudly while swaying from side to side.

4. Gray squirrels have gray fur on their backs and whitish fur on their underparts. They build nests of leaves and twigs in the forks of trees and use these for shelter during the winter and as a place to rear their young.

5. Great tits feed on all sorts of food, from insects and worms to fruits, seeds and nuts. They use their strong beaks to break open nutshells and pry seeds from pinecones.

6. Fox. Most foxes rest during the day and hunt for their food at night, using their sharp eyesight and powerful sense of smell to catch small mammals, reptiles and large insects. In towns and cities they will also scavenge for food in garbage cans and at dumps.

7. Hedgehogs have been around since prehistoric times, protected from their enemies by a coat of sharp spines. If attacked, the hedgehog will roll into a spiny ball until the danger has passed.

8. Stag beetle. One of the largest European beetles, only the male stag beetle possesses the large antler-like jaws which give rise to its name. The female's jaws are much smaller but can actually give a more painful bite!

9. Wood mouse. These shy rodents make their grass nests in the roots of trees, emerging at night to hunt for food. They use their sharp front teeth to break into the shells of nuts and also feed on insects, seeds and berries.

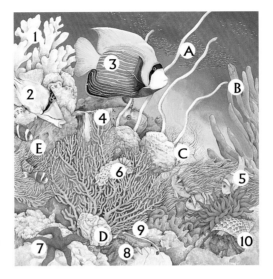

THE CORAL REEF

Danger
ON THE REEF

The hidden animals

A. Blue shark females can give birth to as many as 60 live young at a time.

B. Moray eels can deliver a savage bite, thanks to their strong, sharp teeth.

C. Stingrays are named for the poisonous spine near the base of their tail.

D. Octopuses use suckers on their arms both to move and to seize their prey.

E. Jellyfish. The jellyfish's trailing tentacles contain hundreds of stinging cells.

What else can you see?

1. Coral. Coral reefs are like underwater jungles, supporting over 30% of all the world's fish. They are created from the remains of coral polyps – tiny animals similar to sea anemones – and many have been in existence for over 500 million years. Corals come in all sorts of different sizes and shapes, often with descriptive names such as brain, lettuce, staghorn, feather or fan.

2. Picasso triggerfish. Like all members of its family, when alarmed this fish takes refuge in rocky crevices, wedging itself in by using the first of its two dorsal fins. This contains three sharp spines, the thickest of which can be locked in an upright position by the second "trigger" spine.

3. Imperial angelfish. This striking fish grows up to 15 inches (38cm) long. Its mouth juts out to allow it to graze over the reef, picking out small tidbits from crevices in the rock.

4. Maori wrasse are highly territorial, only leaving their particular patch of rock to search for food.

5. Clown anemonefish have a special group of friends amongst the reef creatures – the sea anemones. Other small fish can be killed by the anemone's poisonous tentacles, but the anemonefish remains unharmed, thanks to a special slimy coating on its scales. It can live quite happily, swimming in and out of the stinging tentacles, protected by them from its enemies. In return, the presence of the anemonefish helps lure other fish within reach of the anemone's sticky grasp.

6. Sea slug. These distant relations of the garden slug come in myriad different colors and shapes, often looking more like elaborate flowers than marine mollusks.

7. Blue starfish. Like all starfish, the blue variety uses its five arms to pry open the shells of clams and other bivalves. If it loses an arm, it simply grows another!

8. Crown-of-thorns starfish. An unwelcome visitor to the reef, this starfish can eat as much as 280 square inches (1,800sq cm) of coral in a single day, leaving behind just a bare, stony skeleton.

9. Cleaner shrimp. This busy cleaner shrimp cleans the bodies of reef fish, picking parasites from their scales.

10. Red hermit crab. This creature takes refuge in empty seashells, moving from one to another as it grows.

Swampland

The hidden animals

A. Salamanders do not have lungs – they absorb oxygen through their moist skin.

B. Catfish use the sensitive whiskers, known as barbels, on their chins to feel for food in the murky water.

C. Turtles do not have teeth. Their jaws are equipped with horny beaks instead.

D. Tree frogs spend most of their time catching food among the branches but descend to water to lay their eggs.

E. Alligator young hatch from eggs laid by their mother in a mound of rotting vegetation near the water's edge. They call out to her upon hatching so she can open up the nest and set them free.

What else can you see?

1. Tree snail. These mollusks were once prized by Native Americans who used their empty shells as a form of currency.

2. Great blue heron. One of the most elegant waterbirds, the great blue heron grows to a height of 3 feet (1m) and is a common sight wading through the shallows in search of fish and frogs.

3. Green anole. To attract a mate, the male anole puffs out his brightly-colored throat pouch. These tree-dwelling lizards have long toes with special pads to help them grip the branches.

4. Cottonmouth. This extremely poisonous snake spends most of its life in or near the water, swimming with its head held high above the surface. Its venom is extracted and used in medicine.

5. Wood ducks lay their eggs in the hollows of trees, hence their name. The colorful male develops his bright plumage only during the breeding season. At all other times of the year he looks like the drabber brown female.

6. Brown pelican. A master fisherman, the brown pelican can dive for fish from heights of 50 feet (15m) above the water. Special air sacs at the front of its body help protect the bird from damage when it hits the water's surface. Like all pelicans, this one feeds largely on fish and can scoop up more than twice its body weight of water and food in the huge pouch under its beak.

7. Roseate spoonbills indulge in elaborate courtship displays during the breeding season, clapping their bills and presenting each other with gifts of twigs. The birds sweep their sensitive spoon-shaped bills through the swampy water, snapping them shut whenever they feel food. Unlike many other birds, the spoonbill's ears can be easily seen as openings on the side of its head. Roseate spoonbills were once hunted for their beautiful pink feathers, which were used to decorate hats.

8. Purple gallinule. This lively waterbird hops across the lily-pads of the mangrove swamp searching for weeds, berries and insects to eat.

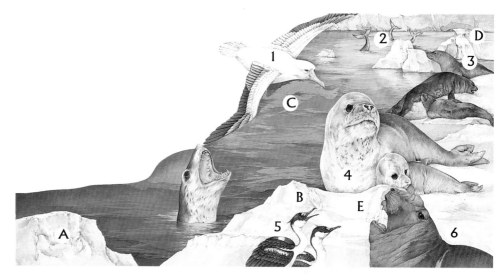

The

LOST CONTINENT

The hidden animals

A-E. Penguins. All 18 species of penguins are superbly adapted to life at sea. They cannot fly. Instead, their wings have evolved into paddles that they use to propel themselves through the water. They spend almost all their lives at sea, coming ashore only to breed and molt.

What else can you see?

1. Albatross. The largest sea bird of all, the wandering albatross can fly for thousands of miles, gliding on the wind thanks to its huge wings. Its wingspan often reaches over 10 feet (3m). It takes up to 10 years for young birds to learn the art of flying and navigation. They will spend this time at sea, only returning to land in order to breed.

Albatross feed on fish and squid, and will also follow ships, scavenging for garbage thrown overboard.

2. Blue whale. The biggest animal to have ever lived on Earth, the blue whale weighs as much as 20 elephants and is even bigger than the largest of the dinosaurs. Yet, despite its huge size, this enormous creature feeds on the tiniest of food – shrimp-like creatures called krill – which it sieves from the water through horny plates in its mouth.

3. Crabeater seal. The most common seal in the waters around Antarctica, the crabeater seal is also known as the white seal because its coat fades to a creamy white for part of the year. Despite its name, it feeds mainly on krill.

4. Leopard seals are built for speed, gliding swiftly through the southern oceans after their prey of penguins and other young seals. They swim around the edge of the pack ice, using their large mouths and sharp teeth to catch unsuspecting penguins as they dive into the icy water. Like other seals, the leopard seal has a thick layer of fatty blubber beneath its skin to help it withstand the Antarctic cold. It can also swim to enormous depths – up to 500 feet (150m) – and remain underwater without breathing for over 20 minutes.

5. Imperial shag. This bird is an excellent swimmer but, unlike many other seabirds, its feathers soak up water to help it dive more easily. When it has finished a fishing excursion, it then sits on a rock, wings outstretched to dry. It nests in huge colonies, building nests of seaweed stuck together with droppings.

6. Elephant seal. At over 21 feet (6.5m) long, the elephant seal deserves its name. Much of its great bulk is due to blubber for which it has been hunted close to extinction. It is now a protected species. The male's extraordinary nose conceals a large nasal chamber, used during the breeding season to utter loud threats to any rivals that may appear.

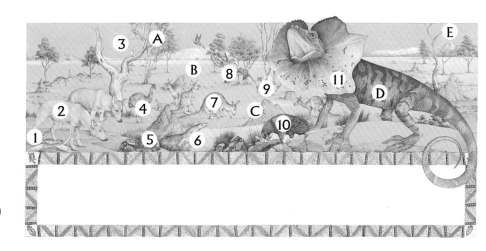

THE AUSTRALIAN OUTBACK

Danger

IN THE DESERT

The hidden animals
A. Wild horse; B. Cane toad;
C. European rat; D. Rabbit; E. Camel.
When European settlers first began to colonize Australia in the 1700s, they brought with them all kinds of animals. Some were introduced intentionally to help with labor (horses and camels). Others, like the rat, were stowaways on board the settlers' ships. The most recent introduction is the cane toad. Introduced to kill pests in the sugarcane fields, it has now become a pest itself!

What else can you see?
1. Desert scorpion. The sting in the tail of this creature is usually used only for defense. It captures and kills its prey with its powerful front claws.
2. Dingoes are the descendants of domesticated hunting dogs brought to Australia by people 8,000 years ago. They have now become wild again, living in family groups or gathering in large packs to hunt their prey of sheep, rabbits, and the occasional kangaroo.
3. Galah bird. The gregarious galah confuses predators by its sheer numbers, gathering in a great whirring mass of wings around the waterholes of the outback. It is a member of the cockatoo family and feeds mainly on bulbs and roots.
4. Emu. Although unable to fly, the emu is an accomplished swimmer and can run at speeds of 30 miles (48km) per hour. The male bird incubates the clutch of nine eggs and looks after the young for 18 months after they have hatched.
5. Carpet python. This snake preys on sleeping birds, mice and bats.
6. Sand monitor. This lizard flicks out its long tongue to "smell" the air – and any prey that may be nearby.
7. Red kangaroo. Like many other creatures of Australasia, kangaroos are marsupials, or pouched mammals. Their young are only partly formed at birth and spend another 8 months developing in their mother's pouch. Expert jumpers, red kangaroos can bound along at speeds of up to 30 miles (48km) per hour and clear more than 30 feet (9m) in a single leap.
8. Budgerigar. Perhaps the best known parakeet in the world, the budgerigar is found almost everywhere in Australia, crossing the plains in large flocks.
9. Brolga. These cranes are well known for their elaborate dancing displays performed during the breeding season.
10. Wedge-tailed eagle. Its 7-foot (2m) wingspan makes this the largest eagle in the world. It swoops from the skies to kill rabbits, small marsupials and birds.
11. Frilled lizard. This reptile makes itself look much more dangerous than it is by opening out a flap of skin around its neck. Also known as the frilled dragon, it feeds on insects.

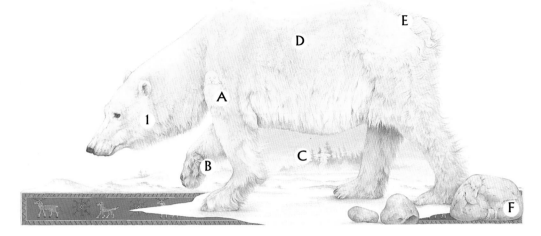

THE ARCTIC TUNDRA
Snow
WHITE!

The hidden animals

A. Snowy owls hunt over the ice for Arctic hares and lemmings, as well as for birds such as ducks and gulls.

B. Snow buntings build a nest of moss and lichen, hidden among stones on the ground.

C. Ivory gulls feed mainly on fish but will also scavenge for garbage.

D. Arctic terns fly from one end of the globe to the other, nesting in the Arctic and wintering in Antarctica.

E. Ptarmigans can fly for only short distances. Instead of trying to escape from danger, they will crouch motionless on the ground, relying on camouflage to keep them safe.

F. Snow goose. Like many birds of the Arctic, these owls use color for defense. Their feathers are snow white in winter to match the snow, but mottled brown in summer.

What else can you see?

1. Polar bear. King of the Arctic, the polar bear rules the northern pack ice with stealth and power. A single swipe from its huge paw can kill a fully grown seal, and a big male can measure 11 feet (3.4m) long. Along with its small ears, furry-soled paws and layers of blubber, the polar bear's thick white fur helps it to survive the freezing conditions of its homeland.

Polar bear cubs are born in midwinter in an ice cavern carved out of the snow by their mother. They remain in this "igloo," protected from the freezing conditions by their mother's warmth and her rich milk. When spring arrives, they are ready to venture outside. Then begins a series of lessons in survival. By playing and watching their mother, the cubs learn to swim, fish and hunt for food until eventually, over a year later, they are old enough to fend for themselves. For the rest of their lives they will be lone hunters, roaming the pack ice in search of food. Seals, hares, reindeer, musk ox and seabirds will make up the bulk of their diet. However, in the summer, when the bears come ashore to molt, they will take advantage of any other food that presents itself, gorging on berries, lichen, and grass, even eating seaweed, birds' eggs, and raiding the garbage cans at whaling stations.

The polar bear has few enemies. In captivity, these bears can live for up to forty years, but no one knows how long they survive in the wild. During the mating season, rival males sometimes fight each other ferociously. Walruses have even been known to kill polar bears with their huge tusks, but the biggest danger of all to the great white bear of the Arctic is the human being. Although now a protected species, it is estimated that over 1,000 polar bears are killed yearly – the world's most carnivorous bear is still no match for a rifle.

INDONESIAN RAINFOREST
Small
SURPRISES IN ASIA

The hidden animals

A. Lunar moths use their long, curled tongues to drink nectar from flowers.

B. Praying mantis. These insects are named after their habit of sitting motionless, their front legs clasped in front of them as if in prayer.

C. Dragonflies are ferocious hunters, patroling a patch of forest in search of smaller insects.

D. Atlas beetles rely on their hard shells for protection.

E. Ants build nests throughout the rainforest, both underground and in the trunks of dead trees.

What else can you see?

1. Swallowtail butterflies all have one feature in common – the long "tails" that trail from their hind wings.

2. Junglefowl. The junglefowl is the ancestor of the domestic chicken, though far more colorful than most of its farmyard relatives. Great flocks of 50 or more birds will gather to feed on grain, grass shoots, fruit and berries, though they will also feed on insects.

3. Orangutan. One of our closest living relatives, the orangutan can reach 5 feet (5m) in height when standing and has long, powerful arms that reach almost to the ground. It uses these to swing high above the rainforest floor, traveling from branch to branch in search of its main food of fruit and leaves. Orangutans sleep high in the branches, too, on a platform made of sticks. Their name means "man of the woods" in Malay.

4. Malayan tapir. This shy, solitary creature belongs to the same order of animals as horses and rhinos. It comes out only at night to feed on the tender shoots, buds and fruit of the rainforest plants. It is a good swimmer and will often head for water if alarmed.

5. Tiger. The majestic tiger is the largest of all the world's cats. Its striped coat helps camouflage it amongst the undergrowth where it will stealthily hunt its prey of wild pigs, deer and cattle. Tigers are accomplished climbers, swimmers and runners, but none of these skills have protected them from near extinction. All races of tiger are threatened, both by hunters and by the destruction of their forest homes.

6. Proboscis monkey. Like the tapir, the male proboscis monkey has a specialized nose. It acts as a loudspeaker for his calls, warning other monkeys of danger.

7. Mangrove snakes have venomous fangs that carry poison from a gland above their jaw into their prey. They glide along the branches hunting for birds, but will slither to the ground to hunt for mice.

8. Egret. Like other herons, the egret is a master of patience, standing motionless in the shallows or slowly stalking its prey of fish, mollusks, insects and small mammals.

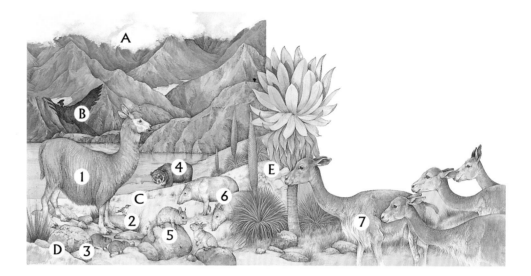

Land

OF THE CONDOR

The hidden animals

A-E. Condors are the largest birds of prey, with a wingspan that can reach 10 feet (3m). They soar above the ground searching for their food of carrion (dead meat) and can sometimes eat so much that they are unable to take off from level ground!

What else can you see?

1. Alpaca. This relative of the camel has a thick, woolly coat to help it withstand the snow and ice of its mountain habitat. For centuries, people have farmed these animals like sheep, using their shaggy fleece to make clothes.

2. Andean flicker. This woodpecker uses its strong beak to make nesting holes in the leaves of the spiny Puya plant.

3. Cavy. The ancestor of the domestic guinea pig, the cavy lives in burrows, often forming large colonies, coming out at night to feed on grass and leaves.

Cavies are kept by the mountain Indians, not as pets, but for their delicate meat!

4. Spectacled bear. The only bear found in South America, the spectacled bear gets its name from the markings around its eyes. It can grow up to 6 feet (1.8m) in length and feeds mainly on fruit, roots and leaves but will sometimes hunt deer and vicuna. Like most bears, it is a good climber, sleeping in the trees in a nest made from sticks.

5. Chinchilla. These furry creatures live in huge colonies, sheltering from the cold in holes and crevices in the rock. Their soft, dense fur helps protect them from the cold but is also the cause of their extreme rarity, since many wild chinchillas have been killed to make clothes. They are now being farmed all over the world for their valuable fur.

6. Andean tapir. A creature of the mountain forests, the shy tapir has a short trunk which it uses to tear leaves from the branches. Like its relatives in the South American jungle, it prefers to live near water. Unlike the dull brown adult, the young have dark fur, marked with yellow and white stripes and spots. This helps camouflage them amongst the undergrowth, out of sight of the hunting condor or stalking spectacled bear.

7. Vicuna. Like the alpaca, this member of the camel family also has a thick, woolly coat. It lives in groups, with one male fiercely defending a band of up to 15 females. The leading male will whistle loudly to warn the others of danger and will vigorously drive away rivals, often spitting at them as part of the fight. Vicuna are very nimble and can run at up to 30 miles (48km) per hour for long distances. Herds of vicuna are rounded up every year for their wool. After shearing, they are released back into the wild since attempts to domesticate them further have proved unsuccessful.

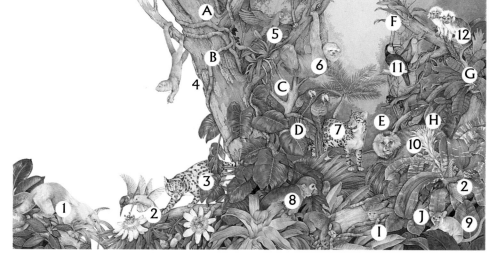

Deep

IN THE JUNGLE

The hidden animals

A. Hummingbird. See 2 below.

B. Snake. The bushmaster is the largest poisonous snake in South America.

C. Frog. Native Indians use the poison from some forest frogs to tip their arrows.

D. Spider. South America is home to the biggest spider of all – the bird-eating spider, which spans 10 inches (25cm).

E. Butterflies can sometimes form swarms of millions of individuals.

F. Monkey. See 8 below.

G. Tamarin. See 10 below.

H. Macaw. See 5 below.

I. Marmosets are small monkeys related to the tamarins.

J. Iguana. This lizard grows to 7 feet (2m) in length.

What else can you see?

1. Pygmy anteaters do not have teeth. They rely instead on their long, sticky tongues to gobble up the ants and termites that are their favorite food.

2. Hummingbird. There are over 300 species of hummingbirds and almost all of them live in South America.

3. Ocelot. The secretive ocelot descends to the forest floor at night to hunt for small mammals. Its markings are so variable that no two animals are alike.

4. Kinkajou. Although the kinkajou feeds mainly on fruit and shoots, it also has a passion for honey, hence its alternative name of honey bear.

5. Macaw. There are many different types of macaw, all of which live in South America. Both the scarlet and hyacinth macaws shown here are endangered, due to the destruction of their forest habitat and the collection of young birds and eggs for the caged-bird trade.

6. Three-toed sloths spend almost their entire lives in the trees – they eat, sleep, mate and even give birth hanging upside-down from the branches.

7. Jaguar. The largest carnivore of the South American forest, the jaguar hunts for its prey helped by its spotted coat. This breaks up its outline as it moves through the shadows, making it difficult to detect.

8. Woolly monkeys have prehensile tails that they use to wrap around the branches like a fifth limb. The underside of the tip is hairless and bears a series of marks like a fingerprint.

9. Woolly opossum. This marsupial carries its young around on its belly, protected by a pouch-like flap.

10. Lion tamarin. Named for the mane-like fringe on their heads, lion tamarins grow to 15 inches (40cm) in length.

11. Toucan. All 37 species of toucans live in or near the forests of the Amazon basin. They have enormous, boldly colored beaks and live mainly on fruit and insects.

12. Cottonhead tamarin. These agile tree-dwellers can leap up to 25 feet (7.5m) between branches, bounding above the jungle floor like overgrown squirrels.